Ben and Pen

Mum
Dad

Mum likes Ben to help.

Ben likes to help!

Dad likes Pen to help.

Pen likes to help.

Is it up, Pen?
L

Yes, it's up, Dad.

Ben likes to help Mum.

Mum likes Ben to help.

Is it in, Ben?

Yes, it's in, Mum.

Help, Ben?
Help, Pen?

No, Dad! No! No! No!